Ultimate FACTIVITY Collection

LEGO CITY

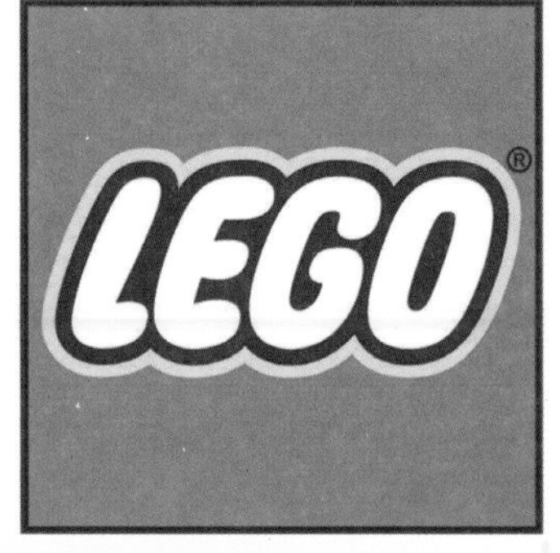

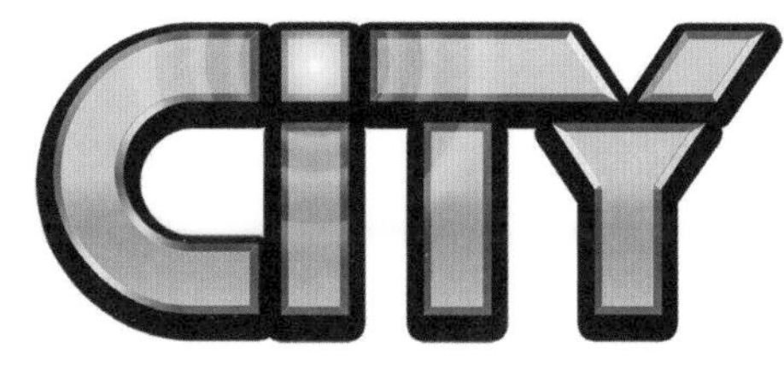

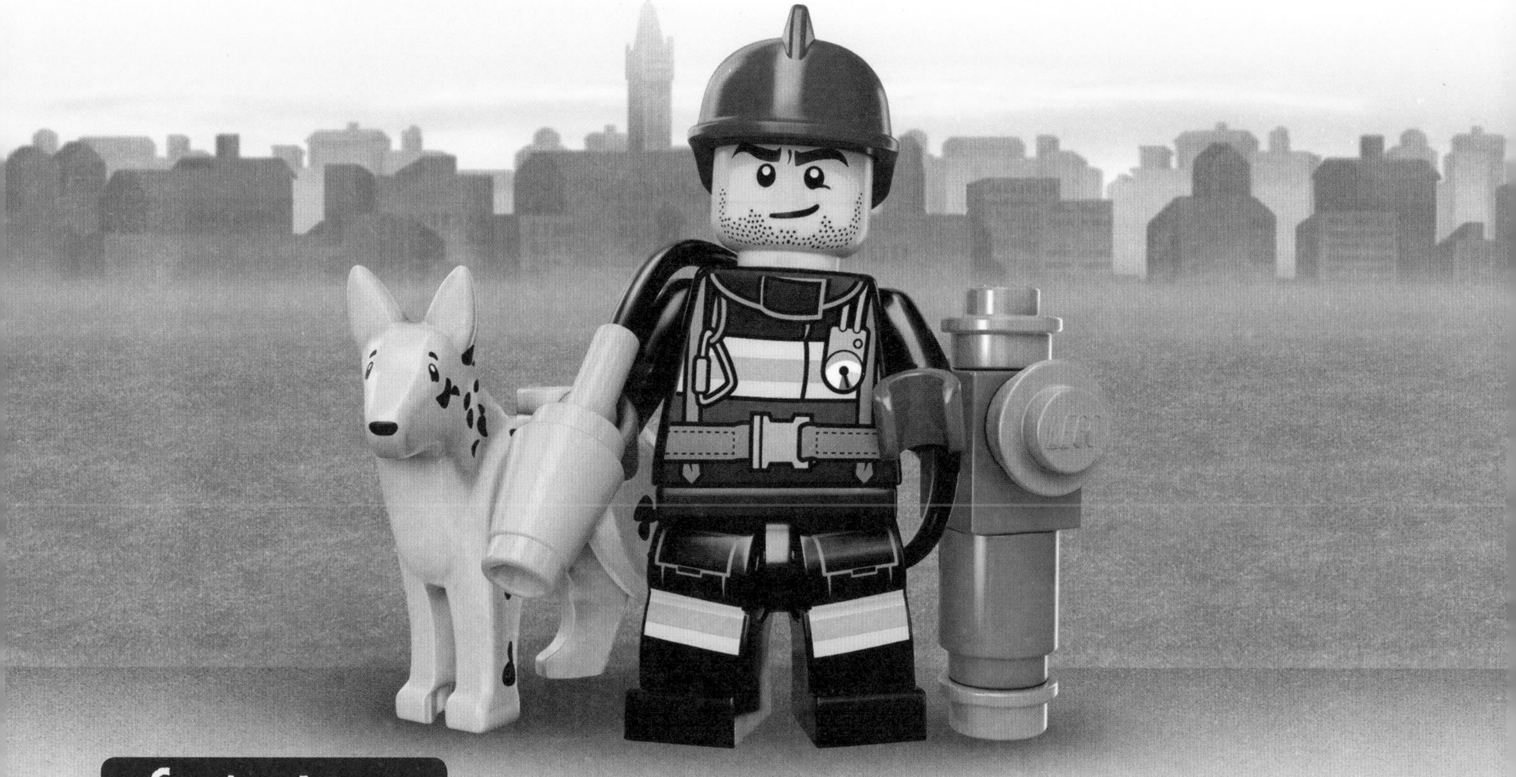

Contents

This book belongs to:

____

Chapter 1

City Life

LEGO® City is full of hustle and bustle. There are lots of jobs to be done – from keeping the streets clean to creating new buildings, and everything in between. There's never a dull moment in LEGO City.

Friendly people

Living in the City is great. Everyone is so friendly and happy. There's always someone around to have a chat with.

On the buses

People from all over the City jump aboard the bus and ride to the Town Square. Some have a busy day ahead at work, while others are going shopping.

New builds

The City is getting bigger! The busy builders are laying the cement foundations for another brilliant building.

Find the **stickers** at the back of the book.

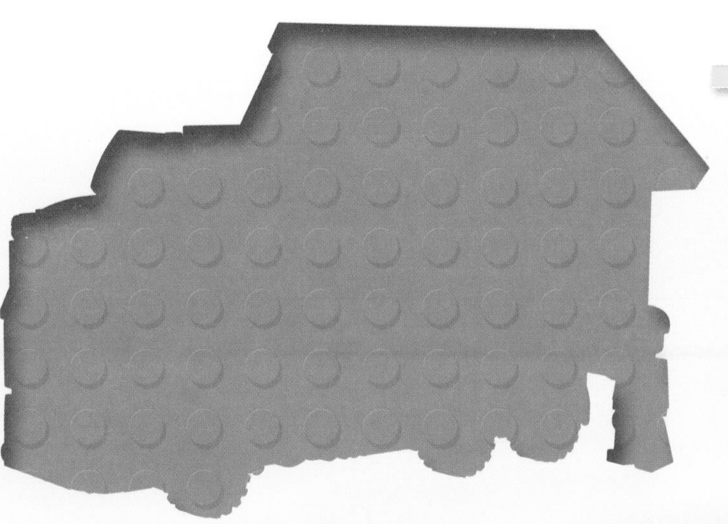

Heavy haul

All kinds of goods are loaded onto trucks and driven across the City. Sometimes they are taken to the airport and flown to faraway destinations.

Spotless streets

Nothing makes the street cleaner happier than a tidy pavement. The only thing that could possibly take the smile off her face is a pavement full of rubbish!

Lovely lawns

The grass in and around the City is always mown to perfection by the friendly lawnmower man.

Safe City

The boys in blue are a reassuring presence on the City streets. Everyone feels safe with these guys on patrol (except the pesky crooks, that is!)

City farms

There are beautiful fields around the City, too. This farmer makes sure the animals on his farm always have plenty of water.

Around the City

Explore the City on the way to the station

There is so much going on in LEGO City that it can be tricky to get from one side of the City to the other. It is a good idea to leave plenty of time when you have a train to catch, because who knows what could happen on the way!

Read the instructions to begin the mission.

The mission:

1. Grab a LEGO minifigure, or something else to use as a counter, and place it at the start position.
2. Ask a friend to join you on your journey across the City, and decide who will go first.
3. Take turns to roll a die, then move the number of spaces that are shown on the die.
4. Be the first person to reach the Train Station.
5. Watch out for hazards along the way!

Start 1 2 3 4 5 6 7 8

The road and pavement are closed while a traffic light is repaired. Move back 3 spaces.

A motorcyclist takes pity on you and gives you a ride some of the way. Move forward 3 spaces.

You stop to help a boy who has come off his bike. Miss a go while you wait for an ambulance to arrive.

22 23 24

Police Station

Crooks that have been caught by the cops are taken to the Police Station. They have their mugshot taken and then they are locked up in the cell. There's no chance of escape with the police dog on patrol!

Museum
The City Museum is home to rare and precious items, like beautiful oil paintings, sparkling diamonds and priceless antiques. It's one of the City's top tourist attractions.
Train Station
The Train Station is always busy with people coming and going. Passengers can browse the shop and buy snacks and drinks at the kiosk while they wait for their trains to arrive.
Luck is on your side! Your friend lends you his skateboard. Skate ahead 2 spaces.
29
28
End
27
26
25
A group of busy builders block your path. Move back 2 spaces.
Some kind rubbish collectors let you hitch a ride in their rubbish truck. Move forward 4 spaces.
Fact Challenge
17
18
16
19
A friendly firefighter gives you a shortcut to take. Move forward 3 spaces.
21
20
A crook is escaping down the river. You stop to watch the police catch him. Move back two spaces.
15
14
13
A farmer's pig is on the road. You help to shoo him back into the pen. Run forward two spaces.
12
11
10
9
Fire Station
When the brave firefighters aren't out saving the day, they are at the Fire Station. They repair the fire engines and check that all the fire equipment works. Whatever they're doing, they are always on high alert and ready for action.

Tools of the Job

Match the tool to its owner

The hardworking people of LEGO City have all kinds of interesting jobs. They each have an essential tool that helps them to do their important work.

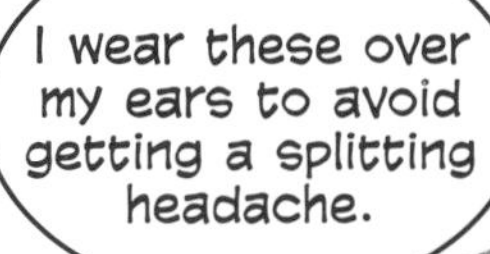

Read about the jobs and work out which tool belongs to each person. Draw the correct tools in their hands.

Lumberjack

Timber! The **strong** lumberjack works in the forest. His job is to fell the trees and then **chop** the logs into pieces.

Builder

This builder uses his tool to **lift** and lay cement foundations for new **buildings**. He makes sure the cement is smooth and even.

Spanner

A spanner is used to loosen or tighten the nuts and bolts on **wheels**.

Axe

This axe **cuts** through large, tough objects. You need to have **powerful** arms to swing this tool.

Brush

This long-handled brush is a handy tool for **sweeping** up mess after an **accident**.

Tow truck driver

If there is an accident in LEGO City or a vehicle breaks down, this tow truck driver is there to help. He **clears** away any **mess** before taking the vehicle to the garage.

Monster truck driver

This monster truck driver **checks** and replaces his truck's massive **tyres** using his tool. Now he's ready to perform some awesome stunts!

Repairman

Broken traffic lights cause chaos on the LEGO City streets. Luckily, the repairman arrives to **knock** everything into place. He gives traffic the green light in no **time**!

Hammer

A hammer makes **light** work for someone who has to fix a problem as **quickly** as possible.

Shovel

A shovel is an essential tool for **carrying** a messy load. It is used by someone who is helping to make LEGO City even **bigger**!

Find the **answers** on page 97.

City Street

Design a new building

The bustling LEGO City centre is where everyone heads for their shopping and dining needs. Today, some new buildings are being unveiled in the Town Square.

Read about the City street. Then design a new restaurant or shop.

Bike Shop

It is hard to miss this new bike showroom. It has lots of flags and there will be a bright, spotlit sign on the roof, too. There are revolving doors and big display windows that show off the motorbikes and clothes for sale.

Manager

The store manager likes to dress smartly. He knows everything there is to know about bikes.

Construction work

The City construction team use a large mobile crane to lift the Bike Shop's sign into place.

Pizzeria

City Pizza is *the* place to go for the tastiest pizza in town. On a hot day, customers can sit outside on the terrace. There are pretty flower pots by the entrance, and the friendly chef always welcomes the customers with a smile.

Chef

The owner and chef wears a white chef's hat and tunic. He serves delicious large pizzas.

Read and Create

Does the **owner** need a special **uniform**?

Are there any **decorations** or **lights** on the building?

Don't forget to design your own **sign**.

What can be seen in the **window**?

Recycling Centre

Find the stickers and the items to recycle

Read about the recycling centre and find the sticker that best fills the space.

The people of LEGO City just love to recycle! It's easy when there are three coloured bins for paper, metal and glass. Today, the recycling collectors have their work cut out for them – a strong wind has blown the rubbish everywhere!

How many paper, metal and glass objects can you find to recycle? Write the numbers in the boxes on the bins.

Forklift truck

The recycling collectors couldn't lift the heavy bins onto the recycling truck without this powerful forklift.

This wind may be strong, but at least recycling is a breeze.

Recycling truck

The bins fit perfectly onto the flatbed truck. The truck has flashing orange lights to warn other drivers that it will be stopping frequently.

Find the **stickers** at the back of the book.

Recycling collector

Once a week, the recycling collectors whisk the bins off to the recycling plant in their truck. First, they make sure every last bit of recycling is in the bins.

Driver

This man drives the truck and forklift. He once found a gold watch in one of the bins. He put up posters and located its owner! What a kind man!

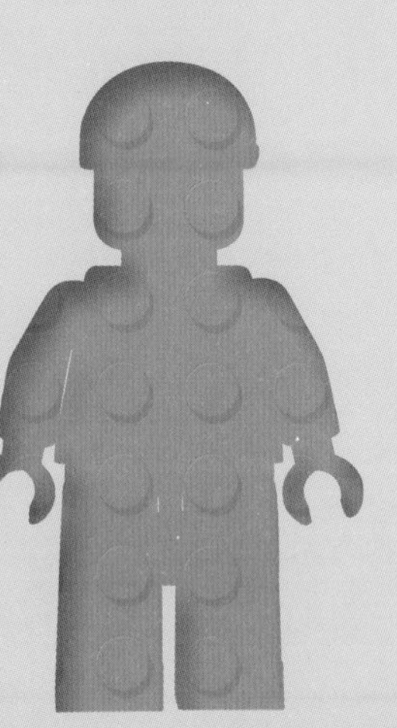

Recycler

Like her fellow LEGO City citizens, this lady is passionate about conserving the environment. She goes to the recycling centre each week.

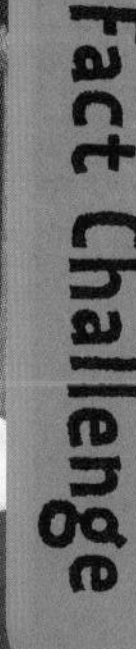

Examples of what to **look** for.

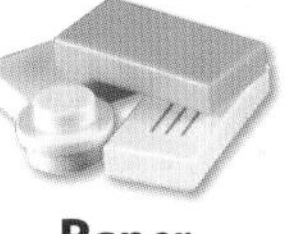

Paper

Metal

Glass

Find the **answers** on page 97.

On the Water

Draw your own comic strip

What better way to enjoy a sunny day in LEGO City than a day trip to the beach! There's plenty of fun to be had on the water, whether you are riding a super-fast watercraft or going for a gentle paddle in a canoe.

Start drawing **lightly** with a **pencil** before you use coloured pens or pencils.

Read the story and then write and draw the ending.

Use these pictures to help you with your drawing.

Day-trippers

Safety first! The friends wear life jackets just in case they fall into the water.

Campervan and canoe

A day trip is easy when you have a campervan. The couple store everything they need inside, and their canoe on top!

One quiet summer's day, two friends decide to take their canoe to the LEGO City beach in their campervan.

When they arrive at the beach, the friends have some tea and enjoy the view – it will be even better from the water!

The friends lift the canoe off their campervan and head out to the water.

They put on their life jackets and set off on a peaceful adventure. But the friends aren't alone for long. Two people arrive in their four-wheel drive carrying watercraft!

Beach fashion

A wetsuit can keep you warm in the water, but one of the drivers prefers to look cool in his vest and sunglasses.

Watercraft

Watch out! These colourful watercraft are made for splashing and bouncing about on the water!

The pair climb onto their watercraft and start speeding across the water. Zoom!

The people are having so much fun that they splash the friends in their canoe by mistake!

The End

Decide how the story **ends**. **Write** in the box and draw a **picture**.

City Garage

Complete the to-do list

It's a dirty job but someone's gotta do it!

The busy mechanic not only fixes the cars at the LEGO City Garage, he helps the people of LEGO City to park and wash their cars, too. The mechanic keeps track of all his tasks by making a list of the jobs he needs to complete each day.

Read about the garage and choose the correct stickers to complete the mechanic's to-do list.

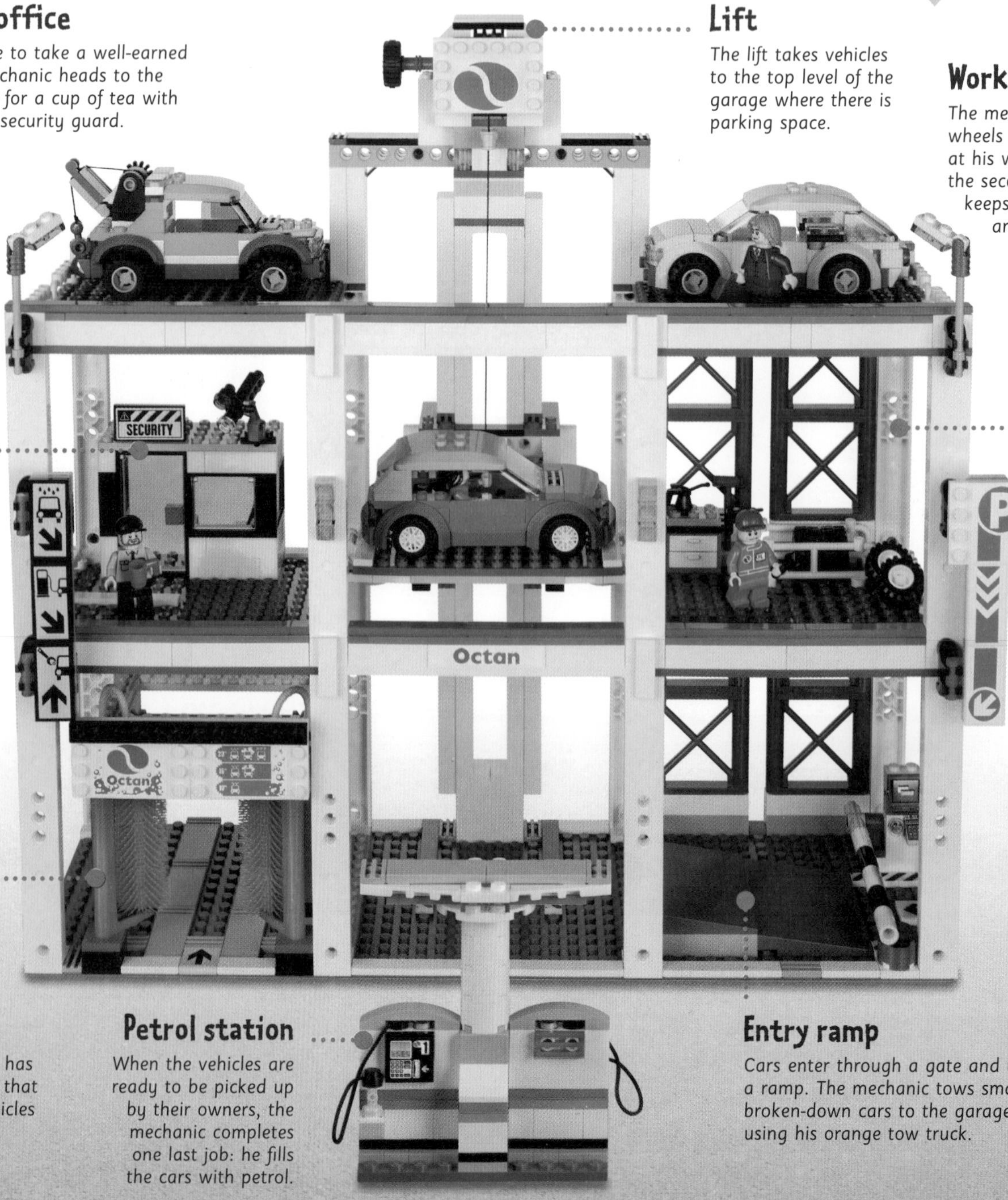

Security office

When it's time to take a well-earned break, the mechanic heads to the security office for a cup of tea with his friend the security guard.

Lift

The lift takes vehicles to the top level of the garage where there is parking space.

Workshop

The mechanic changes wheels and fixes cars at his workshop on the second floor. He keeps his oil can and tools here.

SECURITY

Octan

Octan

Car wash

The car wash has large brushes that can wash vehicles of all shapes and sizes.

Petrol station

When the vehicles are ready to be picked up by their owners, the mechanic completes one last job: he fills the cars with petrol.

Entry ramp

Cars enter through a gate and up a ramp. The mechanic tows small broken-down cars to the garage using his orange tow truck.

Find the **stickers** at the back of the book.

To-do list

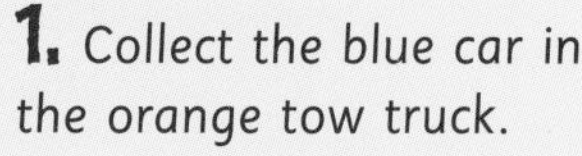

1. Collect the blue car in the orange tow truck.

2. Oil the blue car's wheel arch.

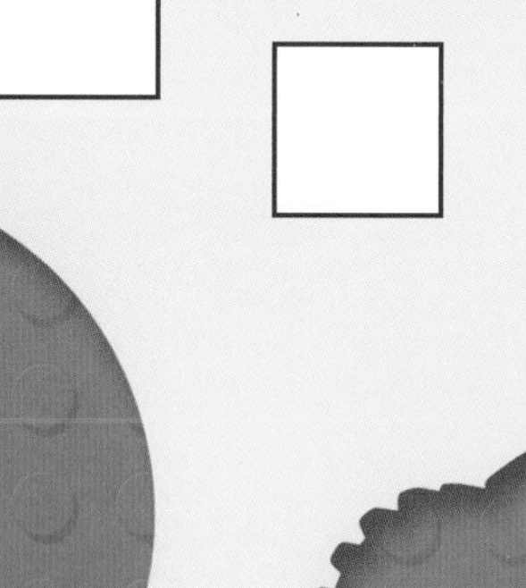

3. Replace the blue car's wheel.

4. Take a tea break.

5. Fill the yellow car with petrol.

6. Wash the campervan.

Put a **tick** in each box once you find the stickers.

City Challenge

Test your knowledge on Chapter 1

Answer each question. If you need help, look back through the section.

Now you have finished the first section of the book, take the City Challenge to see if you are a true City expert!

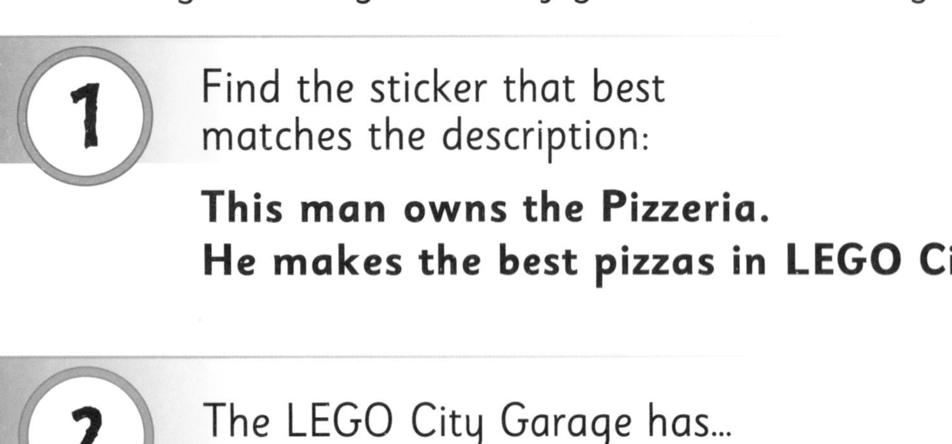

1 Find the sticker that best matches the description:

This man owns the Pizzeria. He makes the best pizzas in LEGO City.

2 The LEGO City Garage has...

an underground car park  **a car wash**  **a helipad** 

3 There is a police dog on patrol at the LEGO City Police Station.

True  **False** 

4 Name this vehicle.

5 The monster truck driver uses a ______________ to tighten or loosen nuts and bolts on his truck's wheels.

Find the **answers** on page 97.

Now you have finished the City Challenge, reward yourself by filling this scene with stickers!

Chapter 2

To the Rescue

The LEGO City emergency service workers are hardworking and brave. Whenever there is an accident, hazard, crime or emergency to sort out, these amazing heroes are just a phone call away.

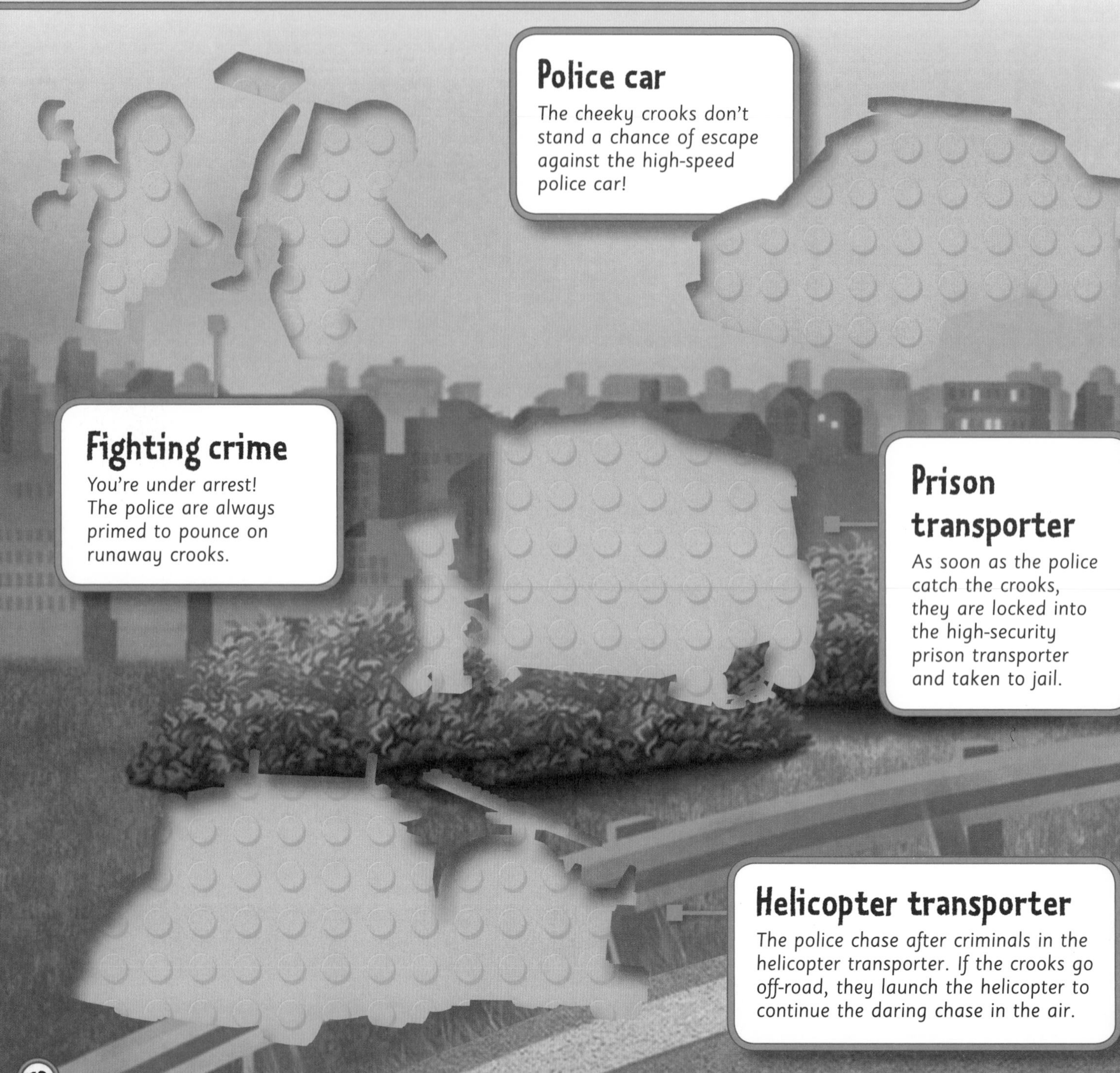

Police car

The cheeky crooks don't stand a chance of escape against the high-speed police car!

Fighting crime

You're under arrest! The police are always primed to pounce on runaway crooks.

Prison transporter

As soon as the police catch the crooks, they are locked into the high-security prison transporter and taken to jail.

Helicopter transporter

The police chase after criminals in the helicopter transporter. If the crooks go off-road, they launch the helicopter to continue the daring chase in the air.

Find the **stickers** at the back of the book.

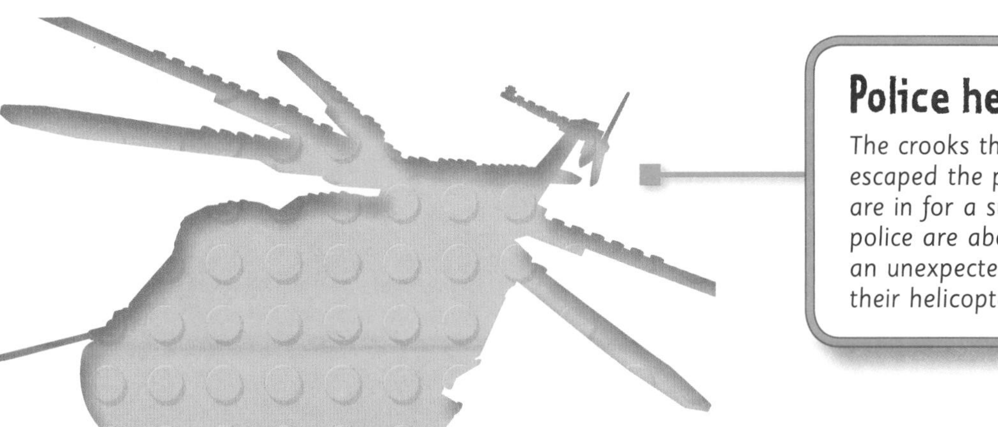

Police helicopter

The crooks think they have escaped the police… but they are in for a surprise! The police are about to launch an unexpected ambush from their helicopter.

Airport fire engine

An aeroplane's engine is on fire! But there's no need to worry. The fire engine's powerful water cannon is capable of putting out even the biggest of blazes.

Coast Guard

Performing heroic ocean rescues is just all in a day's work for the brave Coast Guard.

Firefighters

City firefighters to the rescue! The firefighting team works together to tackle blazes in all sorts of places.

Work Ready

Design a Coast Guard uniform

Read about the clothes and tools needed to do different jobs. Then design a uniform for a Coast Guard.

Keeping LEGO City safe is tough work, but the emergency services are always ready for action in their specialist uniforms and with their essential tools and equipment.

Firefighter

This firefighter wears a sturdy helmet with breathing apparatus when rushing into burning buildings. His uniform has reflective stripes so other firefighters can see him at all times.

Paramedic

It's easy to spot this friendly paramedic in his bright overalls with reflective stripes and blue cap. He carries a stretcher for transporting patients to his ambulance.

Police helicopter pilot

A protective helmet and sunglasses are a must when on patrol in the air. This police officer proudly wears his police badge pinned on to his zipped-up flight suit.

Handcuffs

Police officer

This police officer uses a walkie-talkie to keep in touch with colleagues as she patrols the City's streets. She wears a belt with pouches to keep handcuffs and a notepad handy.

Coast Guard

The Coast Guard keep people and their vessels safe at sea. They usually carry life jackets, diving equipment and walkie-talkies for their rescue operations.

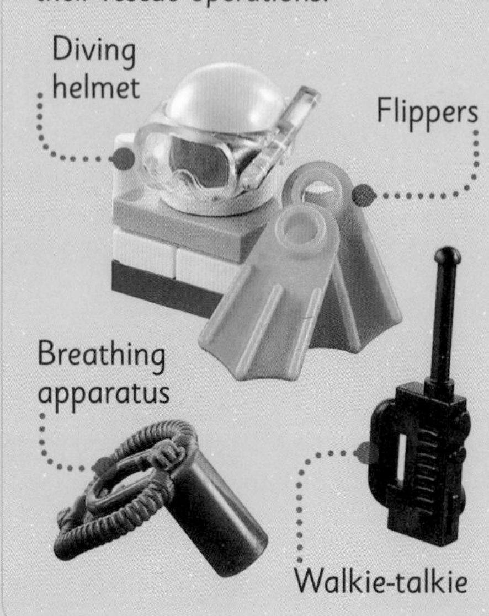

Why not add a **helmet** and other special **equipment**?

Should the uniform's **colour** be **bright** and easy to see?

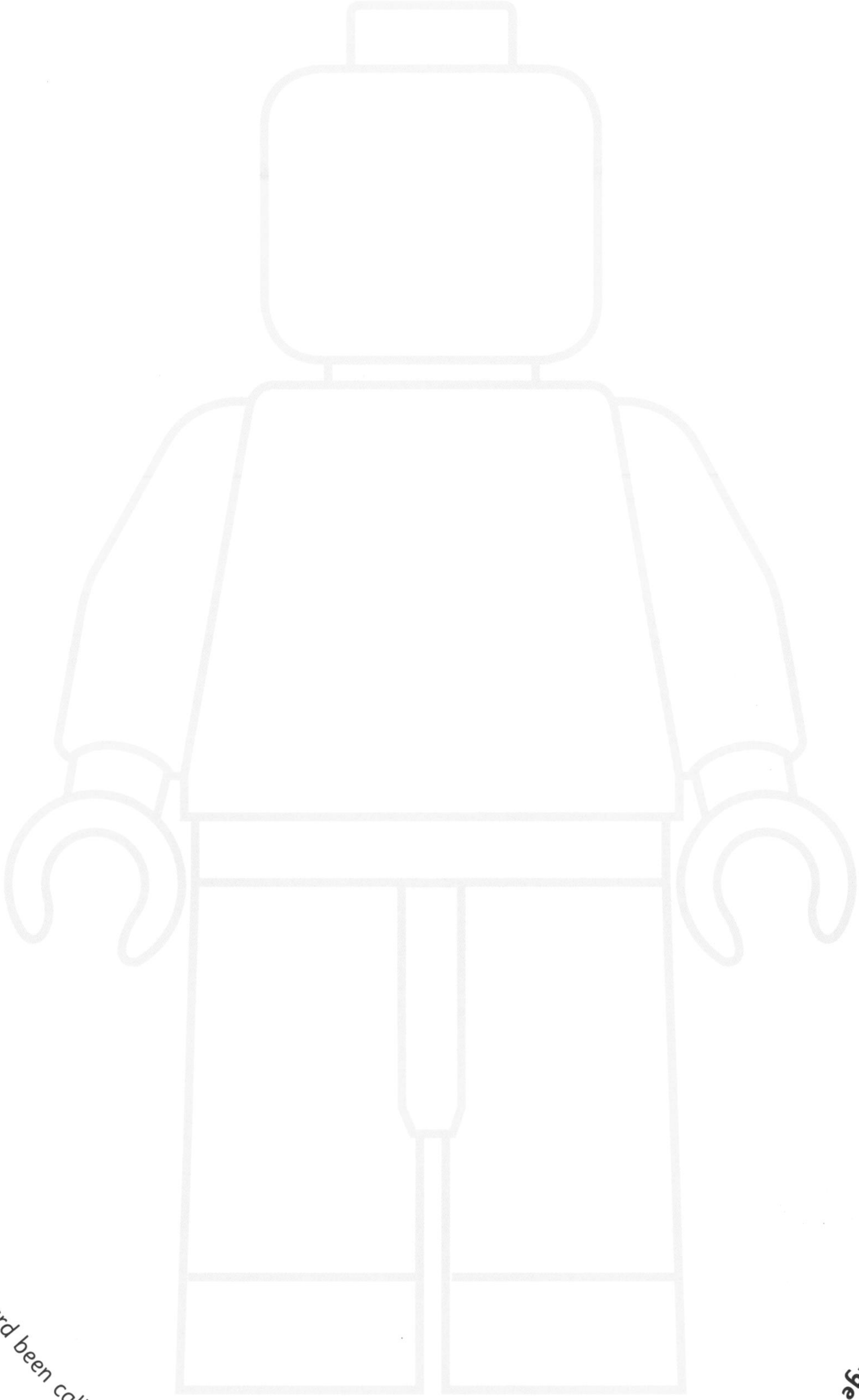

What kind of **emergency** has your Coast Guard been called to?

You could also design a special **badge** or **logo**.

Fire Engine

Complete the sticker jigsaw

This fire engine is always ready to zoom off to an emergency. It is fitted with lots of useful gadgets to help put out fires.

Read about the fire engine. Use the stickers of the fire engine parts to put together the vehicle.

Ladder

This extending ladder is used to reach tall buildings. It is so big that lots of firefighters need to move it into position.

Driver's cab

The driver sits in the cab while the other firefighters sit in the back. The driver has to be very skilled at driving fast.

Flashing lights

When the truck is speeding to the rescue, the blue lights flash. This lets people know they are coming, so they can move out of the way.

Firefighters' tools

The fire engine holds lots of hoses and extinguishers, as well as axes and other cutting tools that are used for rescuing people. The tools are placed in crates and stowed inside lockers.

*Find the **stickers** at the back of the book.*

Hose

The long hose is stored on a reel in the fire engine. It is flexible and easy to control when tackling a blaze.

Wheels

The big, sturdy wheels are perfect for carrying heavy loads. They help the truck get to emergencies in every kind of weather.

Find the **answers** on page 97.

Stop Thief!

Design a wanted poster

The cops in LEGO City's police force are dedicated to their investigations. No brick is left unturned while they hunt for clues and interview witnesses. Luckily, the latest silly crook has already been spotted by half the City's citizens!

Mobile police unit

The mobile unit has everything the police need to start their investigation. Once they know what the villain looks like, they can use their surveillance screens to search LEGO City for the crook!

I saw him! He has a scar on his right cheek.

Me too! He has brown hair with spikes at the front.

Great work, citizens of LEGO City. Now I can file my report!

He is wearing a blue vest and he has a big tattoo of a lion on his left arm.

One of his front teeth is missing and he's wearing a gold belt.

He went that way! He has a bushy moustache and long sideburns.

Read the witnesses' reports, and then complete the Wanted poster.

WANTED

Draw the criminal based on the witnesses' reports.

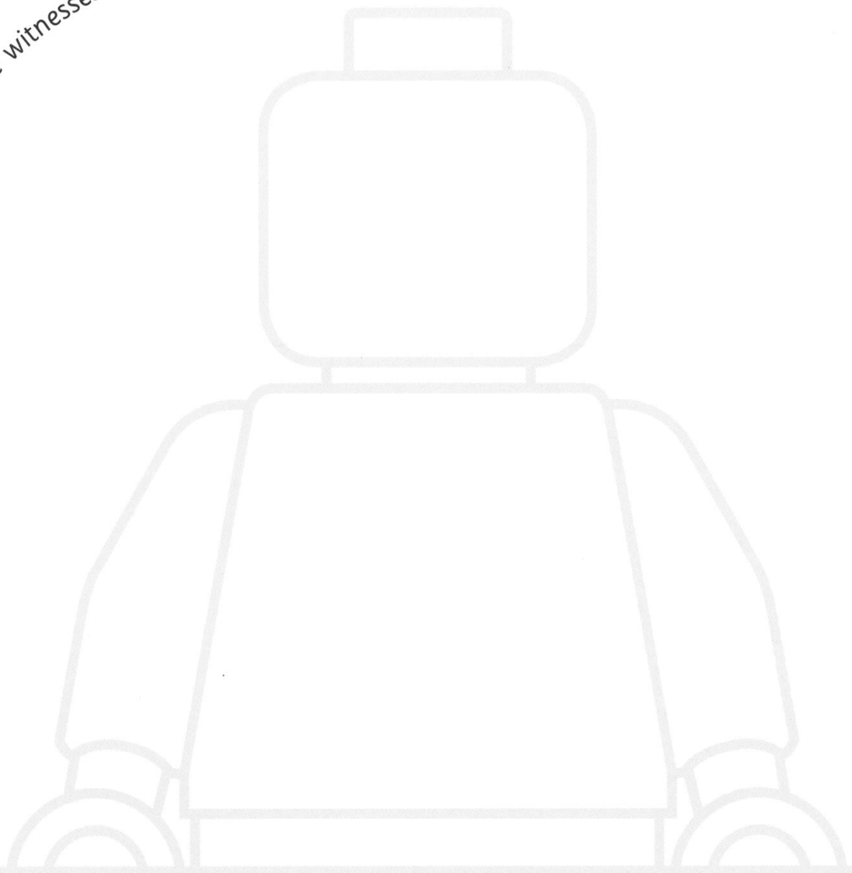

A crook has broken out from prison and is hiding in LEGO City! He has ✎ ______________ hair with ✎ ______________ at the front. He has a scar on his ✎ ______________ cheek and a large tattoo of a ✎ ____________ on his arm. Any sightings must be reported to the LEGO City Police immediately.

REWARD: £10,000

Find the **answers** on page 97.

Clever Cops

Choose the right equipment

The LEGO City police are a talented bunch – they are always one step ahead of the City's criminals. They have all kinds of vehicles and equipment to catch the sneaky crooks and restore peace and order to the City's streets.

Work out which equipment the cops would use to catch the crooks in each situation, then find the correct sticker.

Crooks' hideout

*The crooks have escaped to their **hideout** on the outskirts of the City with a stash of stolen goods.*

Museum break-in

*In a daring **midnight** raid, burglars have broken into the City museum and are trying to make a quick getaway with precious gold.*

Equipment

Spike strip

A spike strip is rolled across a road to make crooks' getaway cars spin out of control.

Police dog unit

The off-road vehicle carries police dogs who can sniff out crooks who are trying to hide.

Helicopter

The police helicopter patrols the streets of LEGO City from the night sky with its super-bright spotlight.

Speed boat

The police speed boat has lots of equipment to catch pesky crooks on the loose at sea.

High-speed chase

The cheeky crook is making a mad dash for freedom in this stolen, super-fast sports **car**.

Water dash

This crook has raided a safe and is escaping with expensive jewels on his **boat**.

*Find the **stickers** at the back of the book.*

Find the **answers** on page 97.

Coast Guard

Write your own newspaper story

Read about the Coast Guard rescue, then write a newspaper story about it.

The brave Coast Guard team battles rough waves, stormy weather and scary sharks to keep the sea safe for LEGO City's residents. From dramatic diving missions, to helping fishermen bail out their leaking boats, the action never stops!

1 Boat trip

- *Two happy* **friends** *and their* **dog** *go out in their* **speedboat** *for the day.*
- *The silly sailors have forgotten to put on their* **life jackets**!

2 Disaster strikes

- *The friends sail too close to the* **lighthouse** *and their speedboat becomes* **stuck** *on the* **rocks**.
- *They put on their life jackets and cry for* **help**.
- *Suddenly, some* **sharks** *begin to circle the rocks!*

3 Coast Guard to the rescue

- *The* **Coast Guard patrol boat** *arrives, but it cannot get close enough to the rocks.*
- *One of the guards* **radios** *the Coast Guard* **helicopter** *for help.*

4 Up and away!

- *A guard arrives in a* **helicopter**.
- *He lets down the* **winch** *and lifts the sailors and their dog to safety.*
- *Hooray, everybody is rescued!*

LEGO® CITY CHRONICLE

MARCH 30

HELICOPTER RESCUE
SAVES STRANDED SAILORS

SAILORS' DOG IS AIRLIFTED TO SAFETY.

HERO SAVES THE DAY.

Think about the most **exciting way** to describe the rescue.

Fact Challenge

Draw a **picture** to go with your story.

Fire Emergency

Draw your own comic strip

LEGO City's Fire department deals with many different accidents and emergencies. Whether it's saving an old building from flames, extinguishing a blaze on a race boat, or rescuing an animal from a tree, everyone can rely on these brave firefighters.

Start drawing **lightly** with a **pencil** before you use coloured pens or pencils.

Read the comic strip and draw in the empty boxes.

Use these pictures to help you with your drawings.

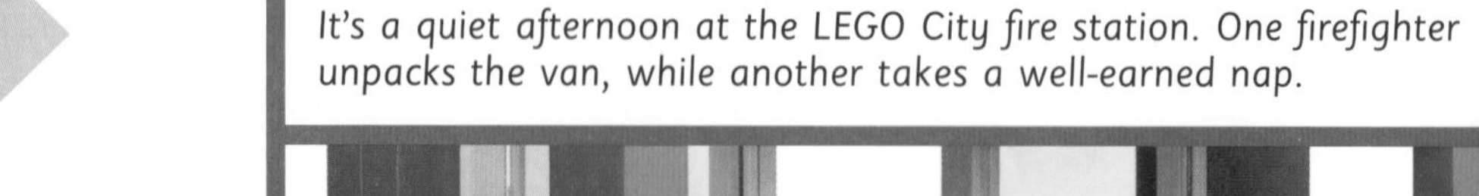

Fire Chief

The Fire Chief has a beard and moustache. He wears a gold helmet instead of the usual red helmet because he is the Chief.

Uniform

At emergencies, the City firefighters wear black and orange uniforms with green reflective stripes.

The phone rings – there's an emergency! The Fire Chief sounds the alarm, and the firefighters spring into action.

There's a fire at an abandoned house! The Fire Chief puts on his uniform and slides down the pole.

When the Fire Chief and his crew arrive at the scene, they find big flames bursting from the roof of the building! The crew get to work putting out the blaze.

The fire is out, but there's no time to rest – the Fire Chief is called to another emergency! A lady's pet cat is stuck in a tree!

But City firefighters are prepared for any situation! The Fire Chief knows exactly what to do... He tempts the kitty down with some fish from his lunch box!

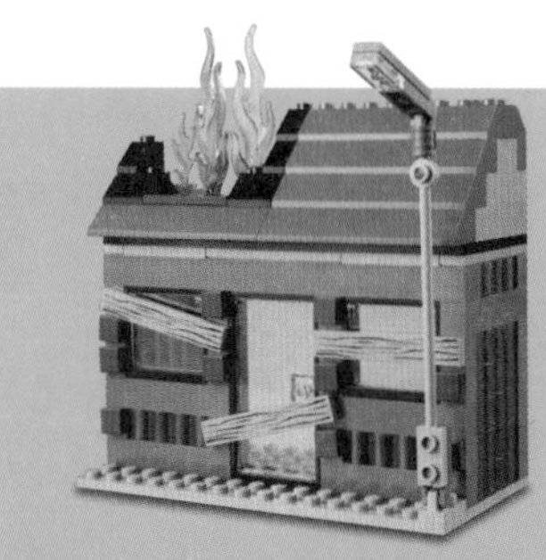

Abandoned building

The firefighters must be quick to put out the flames on the roof of the house. Luckily, no one lives in the burning building!

Fire engine

The fire truck has a long ladder that helps the firefighters get close to the action with their water sprays.

Cat owner

This lady looks happy to see the Fire Chief. He will know how to get her cat down from the tree.

City Challenge

Test your knowledge on Chapter 2

Answer each question. If you need help, look back through the section.

Now you have finished the second section of the book, take the City Challenge to see how much you know about LEGO City.

1 Find the sticker that best matches the description:

This rescue helicopter has a winch to pull people up to safety.

2 What colour is the Paramedic's uniform?

orange ☐ **blue** ☐ **red** ☐

3 The LEGO City Police speed boat has "POLICE" on the front.

True ☐ **False** ☐

4 What is this person's role in the fire department?

____

____

5 The airport fire engine has a powerful ______________________________ on top for putting out fires.

Find the **answers** on page 97.

Now you have finished the City Challenge, reward yourself by filling this scene with stickers!

Chapter 3

On the Move

LEGO City is a busy place to be. Luckily, whatever the City's residents are up to and wherever they are going, they have all kinds of vehicles to get them around the City. The sky's the limit!

Surf's up!

This cool dude can be seen regularly on the shore, chasing the next big wave on his surfboard.

Sail away

LEGO City citizens love to take to the sea. This happy sailor is out for the day on his super-fast catamaran sailboat.

On the road

Many different vehicles can be seen on the City's roads, like this slick convertible. It zips the driver around town in no time at all!

Brilliant bikes

Riding a bicycle or motorbike is a great way to weave in and out of the traffic and to take in all the City's wonderful sights.

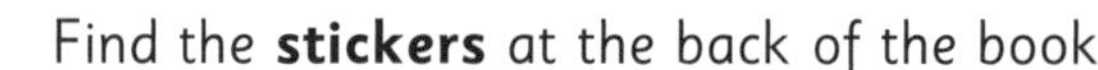

Find the **stickers** at the back of the book.

Soaring high

Planes and helicopters are a regular sight in the City skies, like this super seaplane. It has twin propellors and floats for taking off, landing and floating on water.

Auto rescue

Broken down in the City? No matter the time of day or the size of your vehicle, this heavy duty tow truck will come to the rescue!

Taxi!

Need to get somewhere fast? Just hail a yellow taxi. The friendly drivers will take you anywhere you want to go in and around the City.

Fishing boat

These fishermen load up their boat with rods and crates for a busy day on the water. They know just where the best fishing spots are around the City!

Monster Trucks

Design your own vehicles

The LEGO City monster truck drivers are getting ready for a very bumpy ride! The drivers use their huge vehicles to perform amazing stunts and they will push, crush or climb over anything that gets in their way.

Giant leaps

Monster trucks don't just look very powerful, they also have very strong frames. This allows them to land safely when they make huge jumps over obstacles.

Read about amazing monster trucks, then design your own.

You can use any **colour** and **pattern** you like.

Draw a bumpy **racetrack**, crushed **cars** or other **objects** to drive over.

Big wheels

The trucks have large wheels that are used to crush smaller cars. The big wheels also mean the trucks' frames are far off the ground so they can drive over almost anything.

Spoiler artwork

The spoilers at the back help direct air across the trucks to make them faster. The spoilers are also the perfect place to add fun decoration.

Bumper to bumper

The trucks' large bumpers are used to push obstacles out of the way. They also protect the engine and the driver during daring stunts.

What does **your** monster truck **driver** look like?

At the Airport

Draw the aeroplane's cargo

As soon as the LEGO City cargo plane lands, there is lots of work to be done. The crew at the cargo terminal make sure each parcel is loaded onto the plane, ready to be sent to its next destination.

Read about the airport and how the parcels are loaded onto the plane.

Control tower

Once the cargo plane is packed, the ground crew radio the control tower to clear the runway for take-off.

Forklift truck

Very heavy items are lifted onto the plane with a forklift truck.

Pilot

The pilot keeps track of the crew's progress on his portable radio. He wants to make sure the plane leaves on time!

Cargo worker

The Cargo team pack fragile and smaller items into special crates so they won't get damaged during the flight.

Conveyor belt

There are lots of parcels to load onto the plane. The conveyor belt transports the parcels directly into the hold.

Fuel truck

The Octan truck fills the plane with fuel before it leaves the airport. The cargo plane has a very long flight to make.

Read the speech bubbles. Then, draw the items in each package.

Make sure the parcels are **packed** the right way up!

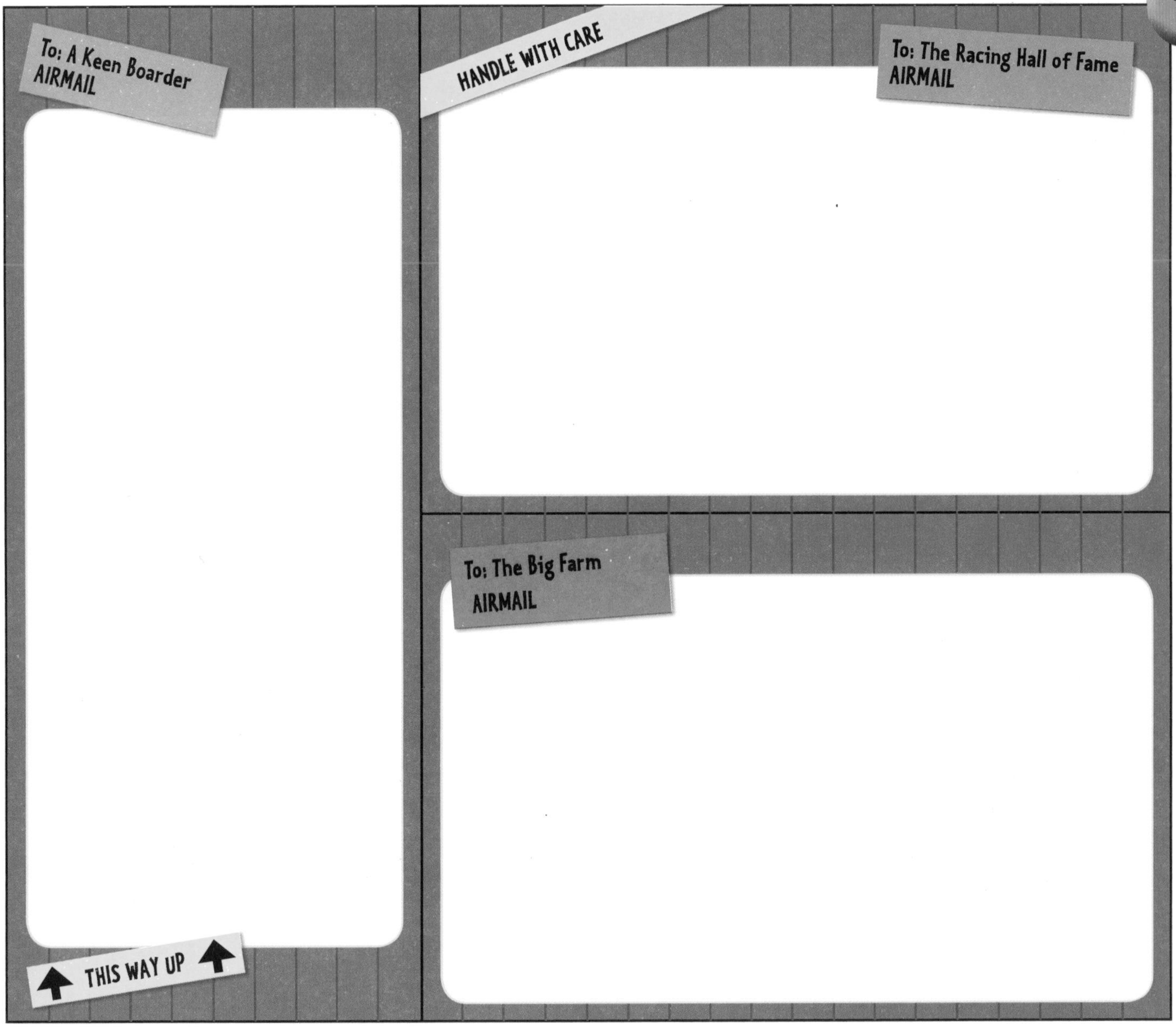

To: A Keen Boarder
AIRMAIL

THIS WAY UP

HANDLE WITH CARE

To: The Racing Hall of Fame
AIRMAIL

To: The Big Farm
AIRMAIL

Why not **draw** other items hidden inside each package?

Amazing Races

Design your own poster

Read about the different events. Then fill in the blanks and decorate the poster.

Whether it is cars zooming across a racetrack or stunt planes soaring through the air, the LEGO City citizens can watch all the fun at the air and motorsports race day.

Stunt show

Is that a bird? No, it is the LEGO City stunt plane performing loop-the-loops across the sky at the **High Flyers Airshow**!

Motor racing

When the start lights turn green, the LEGO City **Drag Race** begins! The race cars speed across the racetrack. But who will be first to cross the finish line?

Go-kart racing

The go-karts whizz around the obstacle course at the **Krazy Karts Rally**. The drivers always wear safety helmets just in case they spin out of control!

Motorcycle rally

Brave LEGO City motorcyclists jump over obstacles and perform wheelies around a special track at the **Motorcycle Rally**. Whoever jumps the highest and performs the best stunts, wins!

Decorate your poster with pictures of the different vehicles.

High Flyers Airshow

Drag Race

Time:

____

Date:

____

Place:

____

Krazy Karts Rally

Motorcycle Rally

Decide when and where the Race Day will take place and **write** in the details.

All Aboard!

Design a new railway

LEGO City's railway is a busy network of cargo trains, passenger trains, stations and wagons – not to mention the drivers, conductors, guards and passengers. Despite the hustle and bustle, the trains nearly always leave on time.

Read about the railway. Next, add stickers to design your own. Then draw in the track between the stickers.

Find the All Aboard! **stickers** at the back of the book.

Passenger train

This high-speed train whizzes around LEGO City day and night, taking travellers to their desired destinations. Whooosh!

Station

All change! Passengers check the train service map and the time on the big clock before they buy their tickets. Form an orderly queue, please!

The track could run in any **direction** and be as **long** as you want!

Train crew

The conductor inspects the passengers' tickets. He also waves his sign at the driver when it's safe for the train to leave the platform.

Platform

There are stations throughout the City. Smaller stations often have just a small platform – but there are comfy seats in case there is a bit of a wait.

Cattle wagon

Moo! Cargo trains move the farmers' cattle across the City. This cow is being transported in an open cart so it can enjoy the view during the trip.

Cargo train

Animals and people aren't the only things to be transported across the city. Cargo trains pull big wagons full of anything from fuel to building material.

Where do you want to put the stickers of the **stations** and **trains**?

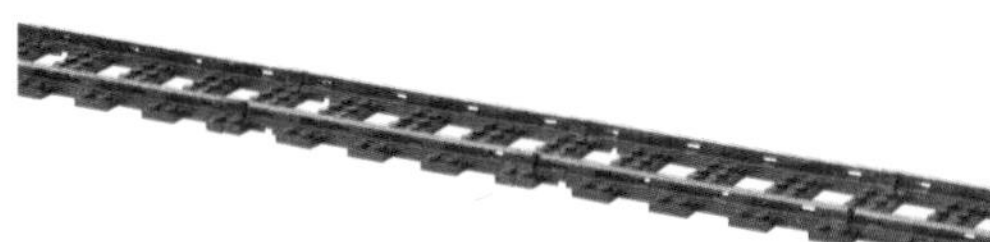

Use a **pen** or **pencil** to draw the **track** between the stickers.

Keep on Trucking

Spot the truckers and their trucks

The people of LEGO City keep moving thanks to these hardworking truckers in their trucks. They work tirelessly to transport essential goods across the city or to drive to the latest traffic emergencies.

Read about the trucks. Then use the clues to identify the truckers and their trucks.

Tanker truck

The petrol delivery guy delivers petrol to all the petrol stations in LEGO City. He connects his tanker truck's yellow hose to the petrol pumps to fill them up. When he has finished, he climbs the ladder at the back to close the fuel valve.

Light repair truck

Traffic would come to a standstill if it wasn't for this repair man. The light repair truck's crane arm lifts him into position while he replaces the traffic lights. Caution stripes and lights warn other drivers to steer around him.

Tow truck

The mechanic saves the day in his trusty tow truck. The back of the truck tilts to allow a broken-down car to be loaded into place. The mechanic then delivers it to the nearest garage.

Logging truck

The lumberjack clears the path with his logging truck. The truck's grabber arm can lift even the chunkiest and heaviest logs. The logs are then chained into place to stop them falling off the truck.

I load things onto my truck.

The truck has a grabber arm at the back.

My truck has chains to hold goods in place.

Find **stickers** of the **truckers** at the back of the book.

1 I drive the:

____

____

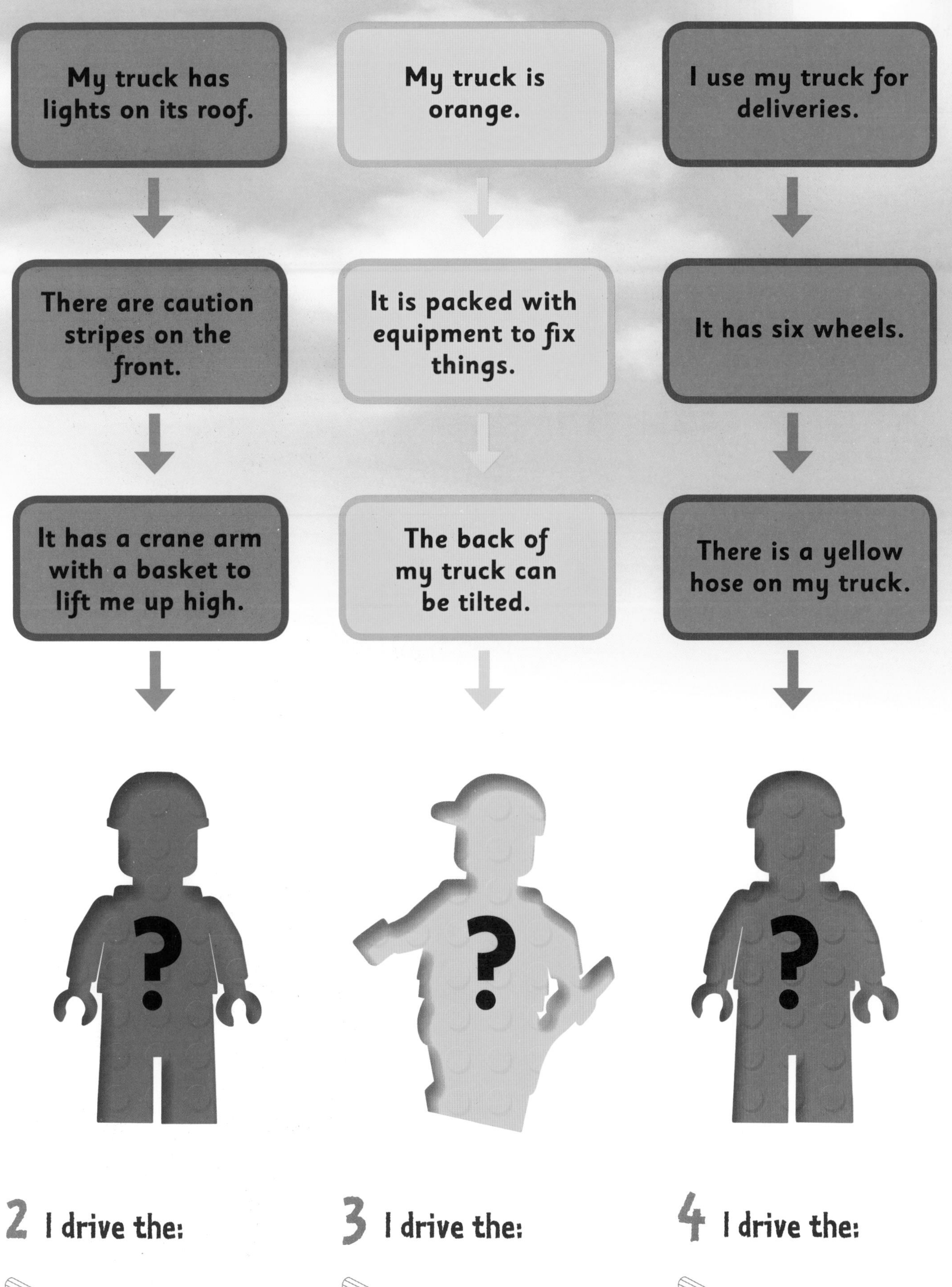

Fact Challenge

2 I drive the:

3 I drive the:

4 I drive the:

Write the names of the truckers' **trucks**.

Find the **answers** on page 97.

Road Trip

Colour in the auto transporter

Watch out – huge auto transporter coming through! This awesome vehicle picks up and delivers shiny new cars to the LEGO City car dealerships so they can be snapped up by eager customers.

Read all about the auto transporter, then colour in the scene below.

Hit the road

The driver spends a lot of time on the road, collecting and delivering cars. He loves his job, especially when he delivers amazing sports cars!

Load 'em up

There are two levels to the transporter – it can carry up to four cars at a time. A special ramp is lowered so the cars can be hoisted onto the top layer of the truck.

Cool convertibles

Sports cars are popular in LEGO City – they go very fast and they look really cool. This businessman has ordered two!

Why not **draw** some more **cars** on the transporter?

Colour in the vehicles any **colour** you like.

Don't forget to **colour** in the driver and the customer.

City Challenge

Test your knowledge on Chapter 3

Answer each question. If you need help, look back through the section.

Now you have finished the third section of the book, take the City Challenge to show what you have learned!

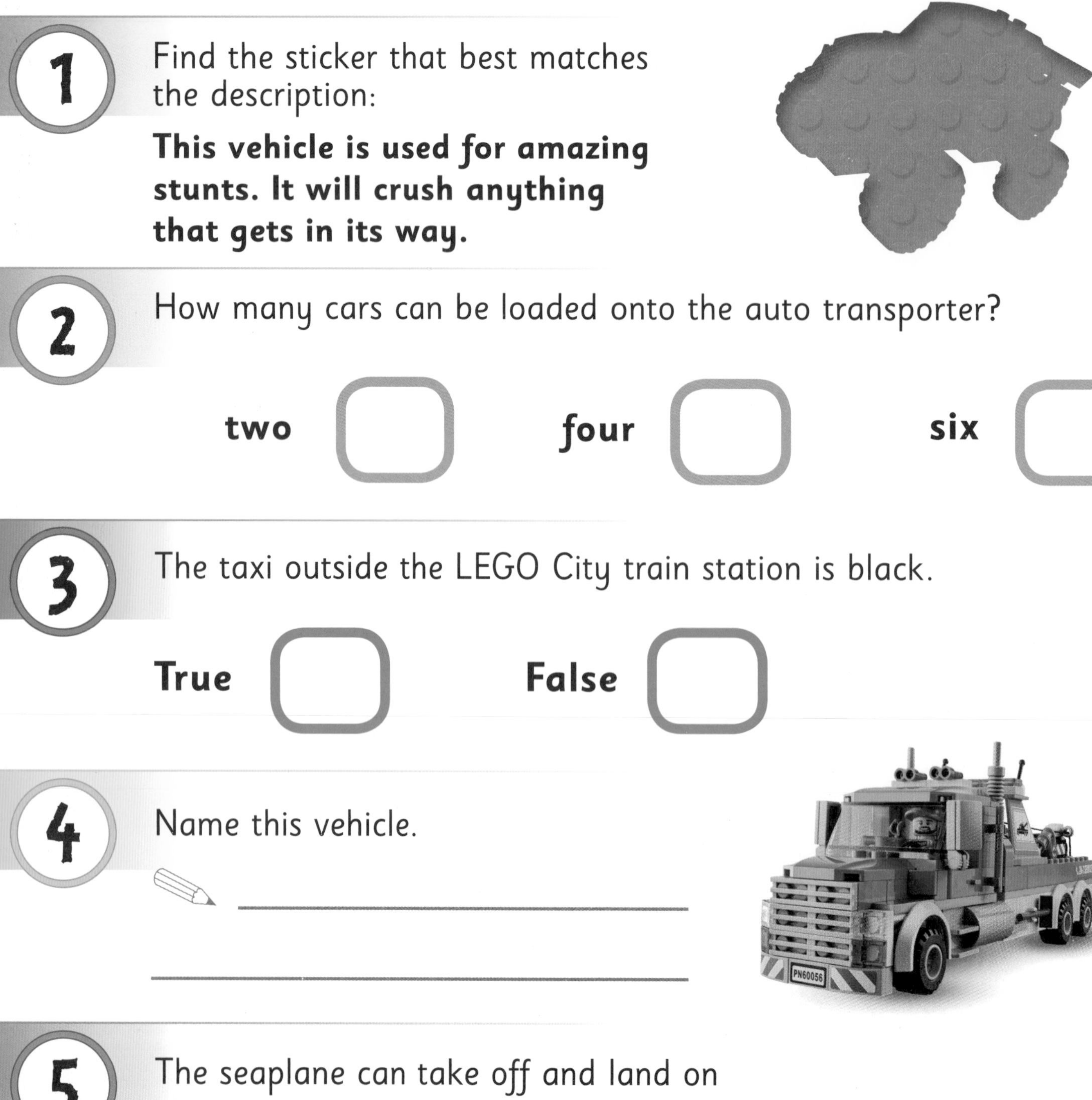

1 Find the sticker that best matches the description:

This vehicle is used for amazing stunts. It will crush anything that gets in its way.

2 How many cars can be loaded onto the auto transporter?

two ☐ **four** ☐ **six** ☐

3 The taxi outside the LEGO City train station is black.

True ☐ **False** ☐

4 Name this vehicle.

____

____

5 The seaplane can take off and land on

______________________________.

Find the **answers** on page 97.

Now you have finished the City Challenge, reward yourself by filling this scene with stickers!

Chapter 4

Arctic Adventures

A crew of heroic explorers, pilots and scientists have been sent to the Arctic to discover the North Pole's secrets. Life in this icy wilderness won't be easy – they must face dangerous weather and tough challenges. Luckily, they came prepared!

Ice-cool vehicles

From helicranes to tracked vehicles, the explorers drive awesome vehicles that are built to navigate the rugged Arctic environment.

Polar bears

The explorers need to watch out – there are polar bears lurking around! Luckily, these large white animals are playful and don't seem to mind sharing their icy home.

Helpful huskies

Husky teams transport the Arctic crew on their adventures. The pack of dogs speeds along in pairs, pulling a sled.

Find the **stickers** at the back of the book.

Mysterious crystals

The explorers make exciting discoveries of strange crystals, trapped within the ice. What can they be?

Scientist

This is a trip of a lifetime for the keen scientist. He carries a magnifying glass and lots of pens for making notes. He also wears his ID badge at all times.

Pilot

This aviator is in charge of navigating the helicrane through some choppy weather conditions. But come blizzard or snowstorm, the skilled pilot always keeps his cool!

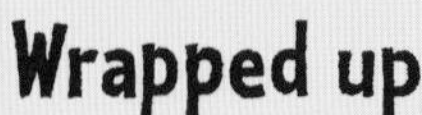

Wrapped up

The explorers dress for the toughest conditions. They wear ski goggles and parkas with cosy hoods, and they each carry a pickaxe for breaking up ice.

Exploring the Arctic

Complete the explorer's diary

The courageous Arctic explorers and scientists live life on the wild side. They are miles from civilisation in their temporary home in the Arctic Outpost truck. There is plenty for them to write about in their expedition diaries each night!

Read about the Arctic explorers. Then, finish the diary entry and draw a picture of the polar bear.

Arctic Outpost truck

This powerful truck was made to take on the most extreme Arctic weather. It has floodlights on the front to light the way and its thick tyres grip the icy ground.

Crane

The explorers bring heavy blocks of ice back to the Outpost, but they need this big yellow crane to lift them into the trailer's lab.

Trailer

The trailer houses a high-tech laboratory. The scientists use the equipment inside to analyse crystals on the lab's special computers.

Toolbox

A big box of tools is essential for an expedition. From wrenches and grinders, to pickaxes and chainsaws, this one has it all!

All-terrain vehicle

Small but sturdy, the all-terrain vehicle (ATV) is great for speedy missions. The explorers attach blocks of ice to the ATV's chain to transport them.

Fill in the **blanks** to complete the explorer's diary.

My Arctic diary

1 It's day one of my trip in the Arctic Outpost truck. We drove to a remote area. The truck's thick ✎ ________________ stopped us skidding on the slippery ground.

2 Then I speeded off in the ATV. I was so excited when I found a big ✎ ________________ of ice with amazing ✎ ________________ inside!

But suddenly, I saw a polar bear right in front of me! Luckily he just seemed curious, so I whizzed off in the ATV.

3 Back at the Outpost, I took a chainsaw out of the ✎ ________________ to break open the ice block. I studied the crystal and then analysed my findings on a special ✎ ________________. Phew, what a busy first day!

Here is a drawing of the polar bear I saw:

Fact Challenge

Find the **answers** on page 97.

Supply Plane

Complete the sticker jigsaw

The ice-cool Arctic supply plane is no ordinary plane. It is specially designed to take off and land on snow. It's a very important vehicle for the explorers – it regularly drops off all the supplies and equipment they need for their missions.

Read about the supply plane. Use the stickers of the plane parts to put together the vehicle.

Find the **stickers** at the back of the book.

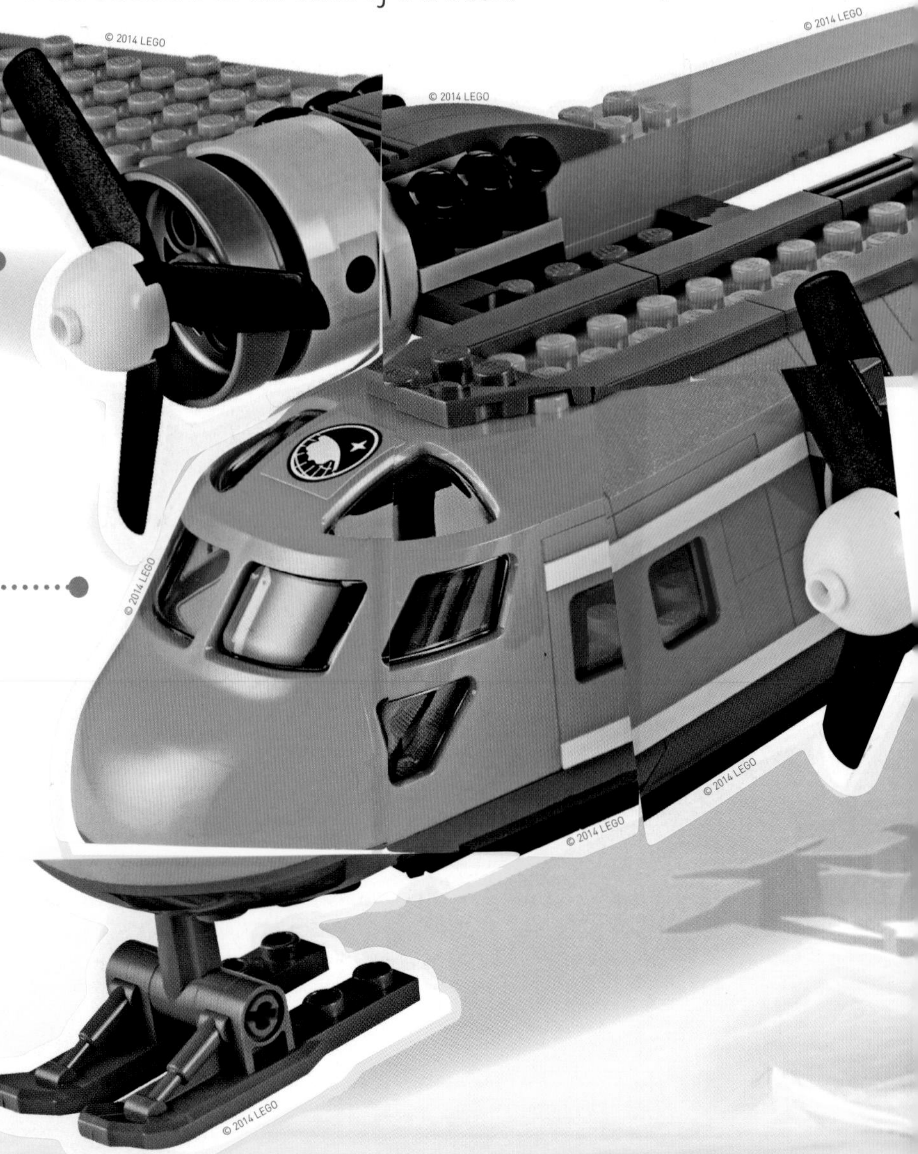

Propellers

Two huge spinning propellers help the plane to launch and move through the sky. The plane's mighty engines turn the propellers.

Cockpit

The pilot sits at the controls in the cockpit. The cockpit has a computer dashboard and dual seats for another crew member to help the pilot to navigate.

Cargo hold

All the equipment the explorers need is loaded into the rear cargo compartment. There are gas cylinders and oil drums for running the Arctic vehicles and base camp, plus crates containing tools and food. Exploring is hungry work!

Tailplane

The tailplane makes the plane easier to control. This is especially important when flying through bad Arctic storms.

Skis

The awesome skis at the front and the sides of the plane ensure that it has a super-smooth landing in snowy and icy conditions.

Wings

The plane has a red light on the left wing and a green light on the right, so other pilots can tell if the plane is heading towards or away from them.

Find the **answers** on page 97.

Arctic Blizzard

Complete the pictures

An icy blast of frosty air can blow in over the Arctic and cover everything with snow at any moment. Luckily, the brave Arctic crew have the perfect tools to help them explore.

Read about the crew, then draw and colour in the parts hidden by the blizzard.

Chainsaw

When the explorers detect something with their scanners, it's time to get to work digging and cutting through the ice!

Scanner

The snow may be falling thick and fast, but there's still a way to investigate the ice – the explorer uses a scanner to detect items buried in the snow.

Ice crystals

This explorer has made an exciting discovery! He uses his pickaxe to chip away at the ice to reach a frozen surprise.

Snowmobile

The best way to get about on a very blustery day is to speed across the snow on a vehicle that has its own set of skis.

Don't forget to **draw** the **details** on the crew's clothes.

Try to match the **colours** with the pictures.

On the Ice

Help the ship return to sea

Getting around when you are surrounded by slippery snow is not an easy task. When it's time for the LEGO City Arctic crew to head back to LEGO City, they use a huge icebreaker ship to make their way through the icy sea.

Help the icebreaker through the maze to the open water. Pick up the Arctic crew on the way. Add stickers as you reach each point.

Icebreaker

The icebreaker transports the Arctic crew back to LEGO City. But it must get to the ocean first! The ship's pointy hull carves through the ice as it travels through the ice-covered water.

START

Base Camp

Brrr! It's chilly out in the snow. The engineer uses the communication tower to radio the icebreaker's captain and waits at the base camp to be taken back to LEGO City.

Helicrane

It's snowing too hard to fly! The icebreaker has a helipad so the pilot can land his helicrane on the ship wherever it is!

Find the **stickers** at the back of the book.

Dog sled
The crew use a sled pulled by huskies to transport lighter items over the ice. The dogs move pretty fast, but they are very noisy! Woof!
Snow plough
This snow plough has large tracks to help it travel over the snow. But it got stuck carrying a heavy ice crystal! The icebreaker will collect it.
Fact Challenge
Open water
The brightly-coloured icebreaker has finally made it out to the ocean – and everyone is on board! Toot! Toot!
Exploration team
Ahoy there! The team members have been out on the ice using their tools to search for ice crystals. Now it is home time!
END

Arctic Base

Design a new base camp

The explorers have brought back some curious crystals to base camp! It's up to the team's scientist to study the crystals for clues in his high-tech lab. The Arctic base camp is packed with special tools and equipment for this important research.

Read about the Arctic base camp, then design your own using the outline provided.

Communications

The camp's radar and antenna make it easy for the team to stay in contact with co-workers and family back home.

Team flag

The first thing the explorers do when they arrive at base camp is raise their team flag!

Home sweet home

The explorers' base is bright orange so it can be seen from afar. It is raised off the ground to make sure it stays above heavy snowfall.

Conveyor belt

Once the explorers have cut open the ice blocks using powerful tools, the crystals are whisked into the lab on a conveyor belt to be examined.

What **equipment** will your base camp need?

Draw lightly with a **pencil** before you use **coloured** pens or pencils to **design** your camp.

Will your camp have a team **flag** or **logo**?

Arctic lab

The scientist and his team use a microscope and magnifying glass to examine the crystals. They have computers to analyse their findings.

Garage

The garage ramp flips down and the camp's snowmobile zooms out onto the ice for another research trip! The garage also has a cosy corner for tea breaks in front of the TV.

Arctic Vehicles

Spot the vehicles

The LEGO City Arctic vehicles are designed to cope with the most unpredictable weather and extreme landscapes. They have many special features for travelling safely on ice and snow.

Read about each vehicle, then use the clues to identify each vehicle.

Helicopter

This chopper belongs to the explorers and scientists at the Arctic Base Camp. It has whirring propellers and a winch and net to carry ice to the laboratory.

Arctic ice crawler

The utility vehicle is great for exploring the parts of the Arctic that are harder to reach. It has mighty tracks for grip, and a crane with a heavy-duty hook on the back.

Utility vehicle

The utility vehicle travels over the ice on tracks. It transports cargo from the supply plane to the explorers' camp on a detachable trailer. The trailer has skis for gliding over the ice.

All-terrain vehicle

This speedy vehicle belongs to the explorers at the Arctic Outpost. It has special rubber-tread tyres that can drive on slippery ice, and a chain to drag blocks of ice back for analysis.

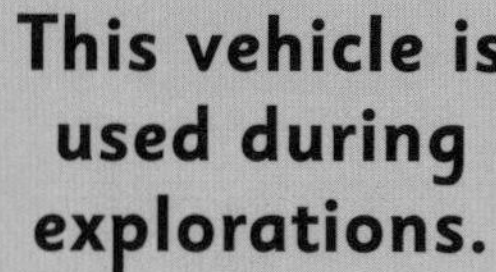

It has thick rubber-tread tyres.

It has a chain at the back.

1 **My vehicle is the:**

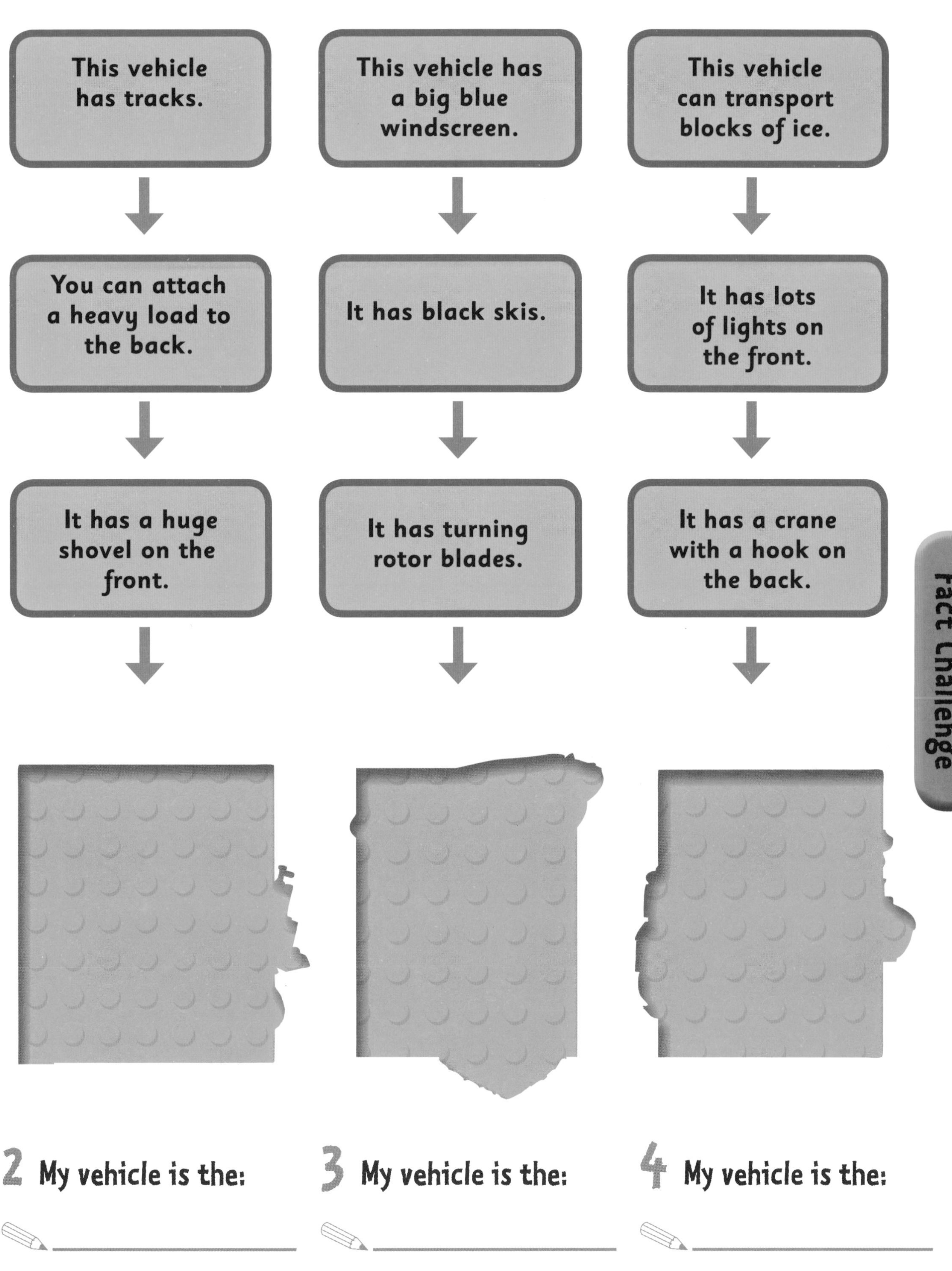

2 My vehicle is the:

3 My vehicle is the:

4 My vehicle is the:

City Challenge

Test your knowledge on Chapter 4

Answer each question. If you need help, look back through the section.

Now you have finished the last section of the book, take the City Challenge to prove your LEGO City knowledge.

1 Find the sticker that best matches the description:

This vehicle speeds across the ice on its own set of skis.

2 How many spinning propellers does the Arctic supply plane have?

one ☐ **two** ☐ **four** ☐

3 The Arctic explorers are transported across the ice by teams of reindeer.

True ☐ **False** ☐

4 What is this person's role in the Arctic team?

____

5 The utility vehicle and ice crawler travel across the ice on

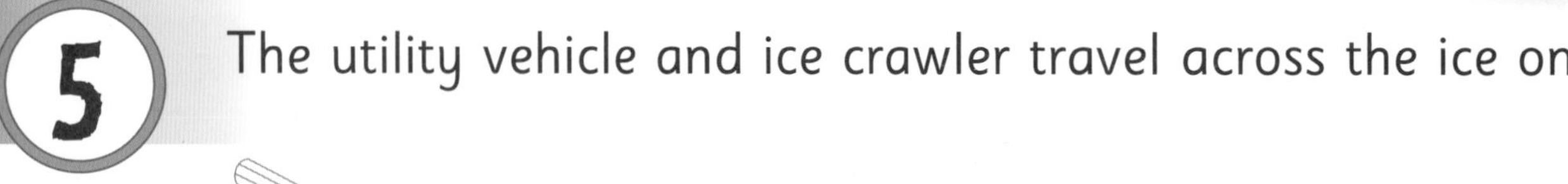

______________.

Find the **answers** on page 97.